Waiting on the Outside

That Monday morning after his arrest when I went back to work—from that parking lot till I got up in that factory, that was the longest—they talk about the longest mile—that was a long, long walk for me.

WAITING ON THE OUTSIDE

When your man is in prison

By Kathy Royer

With Kit Kuperstock and Ruby Friesen Zehr

Photographs by Howard Zehr

Wipf & Stock
PUBLISHERS
Eugene, Oregon

Wipf and Stock Publishers
199 W 8th Ave, Suite 3
Eugene, OR 97401

Waiting on the Outside
When Your Man Is in Prison
By Royer, Kathy, Kuperstock, Kit, and Zehr, Ruby F.
Copyright©1987 Herald Press
ISBN: 1-59244-929-8
Publication date 10/6/2004
Previously published by Herald Press, 1987

Contents

Preface

In 1982-83, Kathy Royer, along with Howard Zehr and Janet Reedy, interviewed and photographed women whose partners were in prison. Out of this project came several traveling exhibits, a drama (which was eventually videotaped), and finally this booklet.

The initial interviews, exhibit, and drama were funded by the Indiana Committee for the Humanities and sponsored by the Mennonite Central Committee (MCC) U.S. Office of Criminal Justice and the PACT Institute of Justice. The present booklet, which in many ways grows out of the experience and material gathered during this project, was sponsored by the MCC U.S. Office of Criminal Justice.

Kathy Royer, who is currently on the staff of the Center for Social Concerns at Notre Dame University, developed much of the material in this booklet. Kit Kuperstock, drawing upon her extensive experience as director of Project Return in Nashville, Tennessee, offered valuable insights and information. Ruby Friesen Zehr, staff member of the MCC U.S. Office of Criminal Justice, served as compiler, editor, and project coordinator.

This booklet is intended for women whose partners are in prison. We hope that it also will help men who are in prison to understand what their partners are facing on the outside. However, a booklet specifically for imprisoned men, *Life After Prison* by Al Wengerd, (Herald Press), is available to help them prepare for life on the outside.

Introduction

The idea for this booklet emerged from a yearlong project called "Waiting on the Outside" in which thirty women whose men were in prison were interviewed and photographed. The women had only one thing in common—they were connected to a man in prison.

We talked with women from six states, from both rural and urban settings, housewives and professional women. The women were at various stages in their experience. One woman was interviewed only weeks after her husband was incarcerated. Another welcomed her husband home before we spoke with her. Some of the women were not married to the men for whom they waited. Others had been married for years. One of the women had met and married her husband after he was imprisoned. All but one of the women had children.

The nature of the project limited this booklet to a discussion of the problems that women, along with their children, face when their mates go to prison. We are aware that many other people, both friends and family, are also waiting on the outside, and that their difficulties are not dealt with here. We are not saying that the situations of those people are less difficult or painful. However, we have chosen to focus carefully on one specific group of people and to share some of the insights that were gained through the "Waiting on the Outside" project.

We are especially grateful to the thirty women who were willing to tell their stories and allow them to be used, along with their photographs, to make others aware of the painful plight of families of prisoners. We hope that the readers of this booklet will find helpful information in these pages as well as new awareness that they are not alone.

Kathy Royer
Elkhart, Indiana

Chapter 1

The First Days

I was pretty upset. I probably should have waited. But
the next day after the sentencing I went up to the
welfare office and I said, "Well here I am. They took
him and now you guys have to take care of me."

Chances are it never occurred to you that your partner might end up in prison. Nobody gave you a book like this ahead of time so that you could be prepared, just in case. It's not something any of us plan for. It just happens.

Some of this first chapter may already be too late for you. Some of these situations may already be part of the past for you. But when you remember those first panicky and depressing days, it may be helpful to know that other women have felt the way you felt then and the way you feel now. You are not alone.

Your Man's in Jail

The baby was crying. I stirred and felt the cold bed beside me. Tom should have been home by now. I squinted at the clock, then was startled by the phone. An accident—maybe he'd been in an accident!

"I'm in jail, honey. They think I stole some stuff. They picked me up with Eddy at his house. I don't know what's going on. I want to get out of here. Just come down here quick and get me out!"

"I can't leave the kids alone, Tom. I'd have to ask your Mom to come and stay with them. Anyway, how can I get you out?"

"Don't tell Mom! I don't want anybody to know. I just want to get out of here!"

The Problem

There's been no warning, no time to plan, to prepare. In a way it's even worse than a death because you can't tell anybody—you're not *supposed* to tell anybody. You feel ashamed and very alone. Police, jail, lawyers—how do you deal with all of these? Who can you trust when you don't even know if or how to tell your friends and family?

You're stuck! The man who put you in this fix is locked up and it's sure he won't be able to help you. In fact, he's going to need lots of help from you. So where do *you* go for help?

Ideas and Suggestions

If Tom had just died, friends and relatives would quickly surround you, bringing food, flowers, and other practical assistance. In some ways jail may be even harder to deal with than death and you need to know that it's okay to ask for help.

Who do you talk to when you have other problems? Maybe your minister can help or else refer you to somebody who understands. Maybe you have a relative you can lean on or a friend who's had somebody in jail. In some cities there are volunteer groups that work with families of prisoners.

If you already have a lawyer, call him or her—it's just possible that they could get Tom out right away. (But don't tell the lawyer *all* your problems because lawyers charge by the hour!)

This is an emergency situation and it's all right to try to call people in the middle of the night. But if you can't reach anyone you will have to wait until morning, even though you and your man in jail are both frantic. Do the best you can and don't give up until you get the help you need. At the same time, don't expect to do the impossible.

Some Questions

•Is Tom telling me the truth? If not, what is the truth? How will I be able to trust him again?
•When can I visit him and what will it be like?
•What do I tell the children?
•What do I tell other family and friends?
•What should I tell the police? Can I hurt his case by saying the wrong thing? What is the *right* thing?

The Police in Your Home

"What are you doing? What's going on?" I cried as three policemen pushed past me and started searching through the bookshelves.

The evening had started out well. Maria and Miguel were settled in front of the TV, waiting for the baby-sitter. Ricardo and I were getting ready to go to a party at the neighbors' house.

Then they burst in! I couldn't believe it! The children came into the bedroom while the police were going through our dresser drawers. Miguel began kicking and screaming at the policeman who handcuffed his daddy.

Just as they were leaving, one of them stopped in front of me and the children and almost shouted into my face, "Maybe we should take her, too. She must have helped him. Did you, lady? Are you in this, too?"

The Problem

You've been invaded! That's what it feels like when the police come into your home to arrest somebody or search for something.

Sometimes the police seem downright rude. If you're not the person they're after, they may simply ignore you, never telling you what's going on. You may want to be rude right back to them. At the same time you may be scared you'll say or do the wrong thing. You don't want to get the person whom they have arrested into deeper trouble—and you sure don't want to be arrested yourself!

All of this can be even scarier for kids. They may cry or carry on. It's hard to know what to do when you feel like crying yourself.

Ideas and Suggestions

You have the right to ask politely for a search warrant and to inquire, "What are you looking for?" The police probably won't stop to answer many questions but they will show you the search warrant. If it looks complicated, at least check to be sure they have the right address!

If it's daylight and your kids normally go outside without you, send them out to play. Otherwise, keep them with you and maybe turn on a TV show they like. It's disturbing to children to watch a stranger with a gun going through their home.

Answer your kids' questions briefly and honestly. If you don't understand what's going on, it's okay to say so. It's important to reassure the children that the rest of you will be together and that you'll take care of things.

Don't argue with the police. You can call for help as soon as they're gone—your minister, parents, a responsible friend, or a lawyer.

It's not always easy to find a lawyer, especially if you feel like all they want is your money. Check with the Public Defender's office. Public Defenders are free and, in many cities, they are excellent. Sometimes they have access to services and programs with which private lawyers are not really familiar. Sometimes they have investigators who are able to round up hard-to-get evidence at no cost to you. In many cities they are more likely than private lawyers to help work out a community supervision program that could keep your partner from serving a lot of jail time. So, before you put your family in hock to pay off a big legal fee you can't afford, get acquainted with the Public Defender's office in your town.

What Happens to the Kids?

"I hate you!" Jason yells out at the street as he slams the kitchen door and kicks it hard.
"What's going on, Jay? Please don't kick the door!"
"That Terry Stone called my Dad a jailbird! I hate him!"
His whole body is tense with anger. His eyes have circles of dirt around them. I try to hug him but he pulls away.
His teacher called today to tell me that he got into another fight at school and she had to send him to the office. I remember that he's been moping around the house, and he sure won't talk to me. Not that I've had time to talk since his father was arrested! Anyway, what could I say to him?

The Problem

Losing a parent is always painful. Children, no matter how young or old, feel that pain. They may feel it even more intensely when the parent has gone to prison. They may feel ashamed and angry. They may be angry at you as well as at the parent in prison.

It is not easy to talk about why a parent is in prison and an angry child doesn't make it any easier. It's hard for children to know how to ask the right questions. And it seems just as hard for you to know how to explain to them what is happening. Their experience is a lot like yours. They also feel depressed and confused. It's not unusual for them to have trouble at school or begin wetting the bed during the first weeks after the man of the house is gone.

Ideas and Suggestions

You and Jason need to have some fun together. Maybe that seems impossible when you're both down in the dumps and there's no time or money to do special things. But how about taking a walk on a pretty day with a stop for ice cream? Or popping popcorn while you watch a favorite TV show together?

What Jason needs most is *you*. When things are this rough, just being there with a hug or a hand to hold may help more than lots of talking. The friendlier you're both feeling, the more likely Jason is to tell you what's really bothering him.

Get in touch with Jason's school. If his teacher and the rest of the school staff seem like warm, caring people, they'll be able to be more helpful if they know what's happening in your family. If you feel that his teacher is too strict and mean with him, it's okay to ask to have Jason transferred to a different class or even to another school. Jason will need all the support he can get—from the school, from you, and from other adults who know him, like relatives or people from your church who understand the situation and care about him.

It's always hard to know what to do about having the children visit their father. There are so many different things to think about. If the kids are small you may want to visit by yourself first, just to check out the situation, at least if you have a safe place to leave the kids. When the parent is in *jail,* visiting is less important because he probably won't be there really long. But a *prison* sentence may be much longer and you probably will want the children to visit at least some of the time.

Just remember: the smartest child expert in the world would have a tough time handling this. If you do your very best, you should feel good about yourself and hopeful that your child will be okay.

Some Questions

•How much should I tell the children?
•Should I take them along to court with me?
•Should I crack down on them or let them get by with things?

Going on Welfare

"I've never had a job," I answer, feeling ashamed. The welfare worker looks at me. I don't think she likes what she sees.

"Before James went to prison, he took care of our finances. I didn't know that he had borrowed so much money. Now I'm stuck with the bills."

"I'll have to see verification of all those bills." She looks at me doubtfully. "Are you sure you've sold everything you can?"

The room is small and hot and I'm squirming. I've never had to worry about money like this before. We've always had enough for what we needed. Now we have to count every dime and I'm not sure I can get a job.

The welfare worker looks at the application and stands up. "We'll have to have all those receipts before we can be sure. You should be able to get some money and food stamps in thirty days."

Thirty days! My mouth drops open but no words come out. I've already borrowed over $200 from my family and I can't go back to them for more! They're so critical—I just can't live on their charity. But what am I going to do? How am I going to pay the rent and buy the food and get the kids' school clothes?

The Problem

Money. Where will you get it? How will you feed the children and do the laundry and drive the car and pay the rent? This problem hits you hard almost the moment your partner goes to jail.

Because it happens so suddenly, you don't really have time to go out to look for a job, let alone a *high-paying* job. Your family wage earner is gone and your income goes down to zero.

It's a learning time, especially if you have never managed any of the family finances. Mistakes are part of learning, but you can't afford mistakes when you are trying to survive.

You hate to ask for money from friends and family. That can lead to bad relationships with the people you love and need the most.

Your kids may start to feel deprived and angry when there's no money to get the things they've always had before.

Welfare may be the only answer for now. But the welfare system is complicated and their people are often overworked. Sometimes it's not easy to talk to them, especially about having someone in jail. If this is the first time you've ever had to apply for welfare, it's easy to feel confused and ashamed. To have to wait thirty days after going through *that* feels like the final blow!

Ideas and Suggestions

A lot of things are coming your way all at once and you could use some help. Talk to a friend or a counselor, if you can, and see if the problems can be cut down to size. Figure out exactly what it will take to keep your family going.

Number one—you've got to have food! If you have little or no income you're probably eligible for food stamps. Let them know it's an emergency and in most states you will get them in a few days.

Dollars and food stamps will both go farther when you shop carefully. Buy basic foods—whole grain breads and cereals, milk (especially powdered low fat), applesauce, potatoes, baked beans, carrots, onions, canned tomatoes, peanut butter, chicken for special occasions, and the best buy available in oranges or juice. Try making some good soups. Have the kids fix their own low-cost treat by popping corn in a covered skillet.

Number two—you need a place to live! That means rent or house payments, utility bills, and the like. Unless you have savings or someone in your household with a job, you will probably need to get help. Maybe your family, a social agency, or a church can help you with these bills for a month or two, until you find a job and receive a paycheck. While public housing is usually the cheapest around, in some housing projects parents say their kids require extra watching to be safe.

Number three—try to keep your phone. You won't feel so alone and, if you're job hunting, employers need to be able to call you.

Number four—clothes. Check thrift shops for good used clothes. They'll be priced low there, or even free, while you have no income. If you can turn up hems and sew on buttons—or learn—you can put together a decent wardrobe for your family at almost no cost. (This may not be true for shoes or clothes for someone with large or unusual sizes.)

If you have children, find out if you are eligible for Aid to Families with Dependent Children, at least until you start getting a paycheck. Some states and cities give additional help while you're getting on your feet.

If you *do* have children, sometimes you wonder if it really pays for you to get a job. Usually, unless you have several very young children, or one who's chronically ill, you're better off *with* a job. Many cities have agencies for displaced homemakers that can help if you've not had a job for a while.

Good child care is as important while you're job-hunting as while you're at work. A grandmother or a reliable neighbor your kids like may be willing to help out. Most of us, though, have to rely on day care. Check it out carefully—your kids are important! Maybe your employment office or AFDC worker can help you get good day care for free.

Other Things to Remember

•Unless you make a large salary, your family may still be eligible for free medical care, even *after* you're working.

•In a big city a car is usually an expensive luxury. If you can use public transportation, or walk, you can save a real chunk of money every month.

•Check out free fun for your kids—playgrounds, public libraries, museums, art, music, and swimming classes. Find out what's within safe walking or busing distance from your house.

•Learning to make things at home can be fun—food, clothing, costumes, gift wrap, furniture, plants raised from cuttings, toys for the kids. Your main limits here will be time and your own imagination. Learning to manage on very little money isn't easy but sooner or later it's a skill that everyone can use.

Some Questions

•How much do I have to tell the welfare worker?

•Is there anyone who can help me understand the application process?
•Are there any other ways to get financial help?
•What should I tell the children about our financial situation?
•Is it possible for me to become so dependent on welfare that I can't help myself?
•Is there any quick way to learn about managing money?

Guilt and Depression

My mind is all fuzzy. I know I have a million things to do today but I can't seem to get out of bed. What's that terrible pounding on the door? Who's shaking me?

"Who is it?"

"It's me, Mom. Where are my clean jeans? I don't have anything to wear."

"I didn't get the wash done, Crystal. You'll just have to wear the clothes you wore yesterday."

It all seems like a dream—a nightmare. I hear Crystal brushing her teeth, but my mind won't let go. I keep going back over the whole thing. Could I have kept all of this from happening? Maybe I should have stayed with him when he was so drunk. Maybe I could have gotten him to come home with me instead of letting him stay with Fred. Is it all my fault?

How can I get going? I have to be in court today. I don't know if I have done all I could, and I wonder what will happen when he has to face the judge. Maybe Larry's right. Maybe the lawyer's not good enough, but at least he didn't make me pay right away.

The Problem

It's called depression and it happens to most women who lose their partners to prison. You are overwhelmed with a tiredness that often makes it almost impossible to do even the most ordinary things. On top of that, your responsibilities are greater than they've ever been before. You're being forced to make de-

21

cisions that will affect the lives of you and your family for the next years.

Part of your depression may be caused by simply not knowing how you will survive financially. Added to the regular bills that are always coming due, you will be faced with high legal costs. You will have to decide how much to spend on trying to help your partner with his legal case. And always, in the back of your mind, will be the nagging question: "Did I do everything I could for him?"

Ideas and Suggestions

Court is scary. So much depends on the judge and the jury. With your partner locked up you can start to feel like everything depends on you.

Obviously you can be a big help. But you're not the one who got the man in your life locked up. He managed that all by himself. Because he's an adult he has to accept responsibility for his own actions. There's no way you can change what he did. You'll want to do all you can, but don't expect yourself to perform miracles.

In some places agencies work with prisoners or prisoners' families. They may offer help with legal problems. They may also provide a range of other services including counseling and support groups for families of prisoners.

You need support, especially emotional support. Maybe you have a good friend you can talk to or a support group in your area. If you keep on feeling exhausted, talk to a doctor.

It's easy to see why you're depressed, but that doesn't help much when you're so miserable you can hardly keep going. Maybe a counselor could help—sometimes professional aid can do wonders. So can some extra sleep and a little fun for you. Go for a walk on a spring day, take your child to the zoo or curl up with a new paperback and a cup of tea. Simple pleasures that cost little and can really pay off in the way you feel.

Some Questions

•How can I be sure that a lawyer will do everything that's necessary?

•Are there business and money matters that I don't understand or even know about? Are any of them illegal?

•How often should I try to see him?

•Why do I feel so tired?

•How can I keep my life from falling apart?

Talking to God

It usually happens late at night when the kids are asleep. The loneliness washes over me like a wave. It pulls me down and makes me feel like I'm swirling on the bottom of the ocean. That's when I pray. Sometimes I stay in bed and just cling to my pillow. I talk to God. I ask for strength and I pray that I will survive this night. I pray for Jim and the kids. But most of all I just cry and pray without words.

I usually fall asleep praying, and when I wake up I feel that God has been with me. I have a special sense of strength and hope that I didn't have the night before.

I haven't been to church in the six weeks since Jim was arrested. I don't know if I could face those folks. I don't know what they are saying about me. But I need God, now more than ever. I need to feel God's presence filling my loneliness and giving me strength. I couldn't make it without God.

The Problem

It's too much. The responsibility and pain are more than you can bear by yourself. But you are alone and there are times when the reality of your situation overwhelms you. That's when you need something to hold you up. That's when you turn to God.

During the first days after the arrest you may find it hard to face people. Even though you know more than ever before in your life that you need God, you may find it impossible to go to church. So you find yourself turning to God in different ways. Maybe you pray more than you ever have. Maybe you go down on your knees beside your bed, just like when you were a child.

Ideas and Suggestions

You don't need to be embarrassed or ashamed of your need for God. Don't be afraid that people will think you are crazy or that your children will get scared if they see you asking God for help. People who love you will know that you need strength from outside of yourself.

Right now church may seem like a little more than you can handle. That's natural and it's okay. It's hard to predict how people who know you, in your church, will respond to you. And going to a new church may be even more scary. So give yourself some time. Don't force yourself into new or difficult situations too quickly. Lean on God and be patient with yourself. God hears the prayers of those who cry out in pain and loneliness.

As you move through the dark days you may find people who reach out to you and who share your faith. Your dependence on God will help you find others who understand your need for God. These people may welcome you into their fellowship. This can be the best way to find a church where people will understand and care about you.

Some Questions

•Does my talking to God mean I'm crazy?
•How can I find people who will understand and share my faith in God?
•What should I tell my children about God?
•Is it all right to be angry with God?

Chapter 2
The First Year

I never cried in front of the kids, and that's wrong. I had to be the tower of strength. I should have cried because at least it would have let the kids know I was feeling awful, but I kept everything pent up inside.

Things are settling out in a strange sort of way. Your man has been sent to prison and your family is getting used to a new way of living. Your new life includes visits with someone you love in unfriendly surroundings.

It involves taking new risks as you work at becoming independent and self-supporting. It means deciding if, in fact, you *will* wait for him. The decisions you make during this time may shape the rest of your life.

Keeping in Touch, Part 1

His hand sneaks under the table and strokes my knee. I look up, surprised. Then I look across the room where the guard is sitting and watching.

"You better not do that, Gary. The guard will see you and then I'll have to leave."

"I miss you so much. Why can't you come see me more often? A lot of the guys have visitors every week. It feels like nobody has come to see me in months!"

"Gary, I can't come every week! I don't have enough money! Maybe I can swing it again soon, after I get my paycheck. But it's such a long drive. I...."

His face goes blank. I can feel his hurt and disappointment. Maybe I should move so that I can be closer to him. But what about my job and the kids' school?

I would like to hold him, to put my arms around him, and know that things will be all right. But it's not allowed and, anyway, it just makes us both frustrated.

Letika is getting tired of sitting on the hard chair. She looks around for something to do. Gary tries to talk to her but she's not interested. "I want a drink," she whines.

The Problem

People in prison get lonely and they need visits. Their days are long and empty. It's important for them and their families to be able to see each other. But visiting is often expensive and upsetting to the lives of families who are living on the outside. All *their* energy is already being used up in trying to live as normally as possible.

Visiting in prison is not easy. While regulations are different in different states, you can't count on much privacy. You may not even be able to hold hands, to touch each other. You can also never be sure how long you'll be allowed to stay. You just have to go when they tell you to. You get uptight trying to remember all the things you've been wanting to talk about.

Ideas and Suggestions

Visiting your man in prison can make you feel like a prisoner yourself. You have to put up with rules that seem harsh, useless, and dumb. You can only see him during visiting hours. You and your kids will be searched before you go in. Usually you can't take anything at all in with you, not even a rattle to entertain your baby! (Most prisons have lockers where you can leave your billfold and car keys.)

Visiting a prison is hard work, especially with kids. You try to keep them neat and clean and well-behaved. Take care getting yourself ready, too. Things will probably go better if you feel good about yourself. You want to look your best for your man. You'll also find that most prison employees are helpful if you make a point of looking and acting pleasant and thoughtful, *especially* if your kids don't act up!

Visiting rooms are often less crowded during the week and sometimes visits can be a little longer. But going during the week means taking time off work and taking the kids out of school. It's a choice you have to weigh carefully. (Children probably will not be allowed to take school papers or drawings into the prison to show their father. They can *mail* them to him, though, in a weekly letter.)

Some things are easier when you live close to the prison. Usually, though, that means a move—a complicated and expensive process. Then, when you do move, there's always a chance that your partner in prison may be transferred to another prison, sometimes even to another state. Prison officials will not check with you about any transfers and you may have moved for nothing.

Sometimes, though, you might actually *welcome* being able to move and making a new start for yourself and your family. Think carefully about what you'd be giving up (familiar surroundings, friends, school, church, job, maybe family) and what you'd be gaining (more visits, less travel time and expense, greater feeling of closeness for your whole family). It's a big decision.

Some Questions

•How much money can I afford to spend on visits?
•How important is it for the children to visit him?
•How often should I go?
•Will he be hurt if I try to explain how hard it is for me and the kids to visit?

Surviving on the Outside

"Come on, Anne. Come with me to check out the class schedule at the business college for this fall. Let's see if we can get enough credits to finish up the legal secretary course. Just think, next year maybe we could have jobs in a law office!"

"I don't know. The kids get home from school so early and Jake doesn't like it when I'm gone from home so much."

"What's it to *him*? He's three hundred miles away and it's his *own* fault! You're the one stuck here, losing out, if you don't get into something for yourself!"

"I know, but it's so hard to know *what* I should do, what I *want* to do! I wish he were here to help me decide. He sounds so angry when I tell him about things I'd like to do. He even accused me of going to school to find another guy! Can you *believe* it?!"

The Problem

You're on your own. You've got to survive. But how? Maybe you don't have any job skills or maybe your skills are out of date. Maybe you want to train for a better-paying job or maybe you just want to improve your mind. Trying new things is scary. It may seem like it takes more effort than it's worth. Or maybe you're just plain scared that you'll fail. You really *are* on your own and it is easy to become discouraged when you're beginning to explore new areas in your life.

Usually, though, exploration leads to new discoveries. Maybe you'll find that you're really good at something you've never even tried before. You'll probably make new friends. Best of all, you may find that you are a much stronger person than you ever realized—and you will survive.

All of this change and activity in your life can also be scary to your man in prison. He may feel like you're getting ready to do without him. He's heard lots of stories from other prisoners about "Dear John" letters and he may be afraid that you will find someone new . He may also be uncomfortable knowing that you may become strong and independent and wondering what that might mean for your life together in the future.

Ideas and Suggestions

You owe it to your partner in prison to tell him what you and the kids are doing. You'd like him to *understand* and support you in some of the new things you are doing.

But some men—whether in or out of prison—just don't understand how necessary it is for women to get training and hold good jobs. You're the one doing the work and paying the bills. You try to *explain* but in the end it has to be your decision. You have no guarantee of when he'll be back in the free world, helping to support the kids. That's what you'd like. But in the meantime, being able to make a living yourself is insurance you need for yourself and your family.

Doing crime, being convicted and locked up, these things don't do much for anyone's self-esteem. Your man may wonder why you'd stay faithful to him when there are attractive men outside who have more to offer. You can understand why he might be jealous.

You understand that and you need to be as reassuring and thoughtful as possible. But locking yourself in isn't the answer. You hope he'll make the prison time serve *him* as he gets new training, new skills, and a new understanding of the future he wants for your whole family. But you're serving time, too, on the outside, and you need to make that time serve *you* as well.

Some Questions

•How can I find out what I am good at?

- How do I pay for training if I want it?
- How can I explain to the one in prison what I am doing?
- What if I fail?
- How will my children fit into my new life?
- Is there anybody who will understand and encourage me as I begin to develop new skills?
- Can my marriage survive if I *do* make big changes in my life?

Will You Wait for Him?

"You should leave him. What has he ever done for you? He's a good-for-nothing!"

"But he's *my husband*; he's the father of my children. I just don't know how I feel about him right now."

"Well, you're a fool if you let him drag you down, what with his drinking and all."

The door slams and I watch my mother's angry back as she walks down to her car. I'm all alone again, wondering if she's right. Maybe I can't stick it out. Maybe he is no good. She's right about one thing. He has caused me a lot of grief. But then I wonder if maybe that was partly my fault. I feel so confused. I don't know what I want. I don't even know how I feel about him anymore.

The Problem

You've been hurt by someone you love and you don't know how you feel about him anymore. Part of you just wants to forget him, to forget you ever knew him. Sometimes it seems that everybody would be better off if you could do just that. And often family and friends, even judges and counselors, will tell you to let him go and build a new life without him. But then you remember some of the good things, like how good he was with the kids when he wasn't drinking. There just isn't any simple answer.

Although other people mean well, they can never fully

understand what you are going through. When you have loved a man and lived with him, it's hard to write him off. If you have children together, it gets even more complicated because you also have to think of what's best for them. Your feelings become very confused.

You don't really know if you love him or not, if you can ever live with him or be a family again. But advice, even from people you respect, comes from the outside. In the end you know that you must find your own way in this.

Ideas and Suggestions

You need time. Your partner has been arrested, jailed, tried, and then sentenced to prison and you're doing well just to be walking around and holding down your job. You're certainly in no condition to make major decisions that will affect the rest of your life.

Let your family know that you love them and need their support but that you don't want to have to choose between them and your man. Let them know how important this is for all of you—for you, your partner, and your children. You need time to work things through without pressure from them.

You're going to be asking yourself some hard questions. Exactly what did your partner do? What was he like in the past? What does the future look like? If he drinks or abuses you, you'll need to get some extra good advice before you decide anything. Most men don't stop that kind of behavior for long unless they also get some help. Maybe you can talk with your minister, a counselor at a mental health center or some other wise friend who can help you sort things out. Usually there's somebody who can help, if you can just get yourself to ask.

What if, in the end, you do decide to leave him? When do you do that and how? There doesn't seem to be any right time. You may want to stick with him through the trial and sentencing. Sometimes that can really make a difference in the sentence. You also probably don't want to send a "Dear John" letter just before he finally gets out of prison. But you want him to know before he gets out. That means you have to be sure about your decision well before he's due to be released. He

32

needs time to get used to the idea that you will not be there waiting for him when he gets out.

And what if you decide to stick with him? While that may seem like an easier decision, it probably won't be once he gets out. Prisons often seem to turn men into children. That's not good for any of you if you're going to remain a family. Encourage him, even in prison, to assume as much responsibility for the family as he possibly can. The *more* involved he is while in prison, the *easier* it will be for him to resume his life as a responsible adult at home.

Some Questions

•How can I know if we can work things out when we hardly see each other?
•How much should I listen to other people?
•How much should I listen to his begging and arguing?
•How normal can my life (and the children's) be if I remain tied to a prisoner?
•Can I bargain with him to go through a treatment program (for alcohol, drugs, or abusive behavior) before he comes back home to live?

Finding a Church

There I was, sitting in a strange Sunday school class. They were talking about helping each other. One woman talked about how important her friends were when her daughter died.

I bit my lip. I had only been coming here for a few weeks and I didn't want to say anything. A friend from work had invited me. So far I had been able to avoid difficult questions. It was good to be able to sing and pray with other people and I didn't want to lose that good feeling.

Other people in the class talked about how they felt supported by others in the congregation when they had problems. Nobody said anything about prison! What would they say if they knew?

All of a sudden I heard myself blurting it out, my words practically tumbling over each other. I told them about Charlie. I told them how lonely I'd been during the last year. I told them how ashamed I felt.

When all the words were out there was only quiet. I looked up and then I knew that it was going to be okay. They began to talk to me, saying they were glad I had told my story. Soon they were beginning to figure out how they could help!

The Problem

You need friends. You need someone who cares about you and shares your faith. Those kinds of people are hard to find. Sometimes you want to worship with other people who believe the same things you do. But it's hard to find a group, even a church, that will accept you just the way you are. It's risky business to tell about Charlie being in prison and what that's meant for your family during the past year.

Finding a new church means taking some risks. Many churches are hard on people who don't fit their picture of what a "Christian" should be like. On the other hand, some churches are places that help make new beginnings possible as you find good friends and begin to find God in other people.

Ideas and Suggestions

If you find a churchgoing friend who is sensitive and caring, maybe you can ask that person about church. Chances are that a person like that will have chosen a church that welcomes people with different experiences.

But go slowly into a new church. Feel your way and pray for God's guidance. Even in a warm church you will need to find those people who can listen and care about you. Not everyone will be ready to hear your story.

Seek out those people in the church with whom you feel comfortable and work at getting to know them. Sometimes it is helpful to talk to the pastor because he or she often has the time and the skills to help in a situation like yours. A pastor can also introduce you to others in the church who might become good friends.

Remember that taking risks is part of growing. So take the risks cautiously and prayerfully. There is no guarantee that things will work out in a new church but there is the *possibility*. And if they do work out, you have gained a rich resource that can help you through the hard times.

Some Questions

•How can I help my children feel good about going to church?
•How can I tell which people will be able to hear my story with a sympathetic ear?
•What will Charlie think about me spilling everything to strangers in a church?
•Could I worship in a church where I have to be careful about what I tell people?
•How can I help my children feel good about going to church?

Chapter 3

The Long Haul

The kid, he misses him—all he says is "da, da," and I can't tell him daddy's coming home soon because I don't know—it's up to the board. The board tells you when you gotta go and don't go.

If you *do* decide to wait, your new way of life can become a long haul. Trying to keep in touch will be an ongoing struggle. The possibility of parole may feel like both a curse and a blessing. It gives hope, only to be destroyed when parole is denied. Sometimes parole may depend on going through a treatment program first.

Life goes on. Kids keep growing up and you can't ask them to put off having a good time until their father is home. Your family time is *now* and you should not feel guilty for making the most of it.

Keeping in Touch, Part 2

"I know you don't want to tell Dad, Margie. I know it would be easier just to pretend it didn't happen. I also know your father would want to know that you failed English and that maybe you won't be able to graduate."

"Please, Mom, just this once, let's take care of it without telling him. You know he'll just get upset. He'll yell when we go to visit and he'll have a miserable week."

In some ways Margie is just like her father, persuasive and charming, but I really don't think we can keep secrets from Donald while he is in prison. Then again, maybe it wouldn't hurt. There's nothing he can do about it anyway. I could talk to the English teacher and crack down on Margie so it would all be taken care of before Donald comes up for parole. Margie's right—it will only ruin his week.

The Problem

Family life goes on. Even with visits, letters and phone calls, it's still impossible for a father in prison to be very involved in the daily life of his family. Often problems have to be dealt with on the spot; there's no time to check first with someone who's locked up several hundred miles away. Sometimes a crisis is over before you are able to talk with the person in prison.

When this happens the father in prison feels useless and alone because he feels his family doesn't need him. He wants to know what's going on, to be involved. But being powerless to do anything, that may just make him *more* frustrated and angry. It's a no-win situation.

Even when you *want* to keep him involved, you and your family end up making choices about what to tell your partner in prison. Your family life cannot stop while you wait for a letter or a visit that is ten days away.

The days and weeks go by and it gets to be a long haul. Sometimes you feel as if you don't have the energy to keep the relationship going and you certainly don't know how to keep your

partner involved in the family. Letters, phone calls, even visits—
it's just not like having him home and you wonder if it's worth it
all.

Ideas and Suggestions

When you only get to visit once or twice a month, you don't
want to use up all your time talking about all the little, everyday
problems. The kids' father probably won't be shocked, when he
does get out, that their rooms are a mess or that they sometimes
lose their lunch money. But something major is different.
Margie's father will have reason to be upset if he finds out
without any warning that Margie won't be graduating this year.
So better tell him now.

If their father sees the children regularly, it makes sense to ask
his advice about when Margie should be in at night, or whether
he thinks she needs her eyes tested. Sometimes he might even
notice things about the kids that you don't see because you are
with them every day. The more he can be involved in family decisions *now*, the easier it will be for him to fit into the family
when he comes home.

Some prisons have groups such as Parents in Prison or MILK
(Men Inside Loving Kids) which can give a prisoner father new
insight and information about kids. A few prisons include wives
in their pre-release programs. This can be really helpful in pre-
paring together for the big transition back to family and community.

Some Questions

•Is it important for him to know all the details of my life?
•Do the children feel closer to him when he helps to make deci-
  sions about their lives?
•Should I make the kids write to him?
•How can I tell from his letters what's *really* going on inside of
  him?
•Should I worry that something has happened to him if I don't
  hear from him?

Parole: Yes, No, Maybe So

"Honey, I think I'm going up for parole next month!"

"Next month! Does that mean you'll be home soon?"

"I don't know. Seems like I'm the last one to find out about these things."

My heart is beating fast when I hang up the phone. Next month! Home at last!

Next month comes and goes. I have called lawyers and contacted members of the parole board but still they haven't decided if he can come home or not. I feel like giving up. I get my hopes so high, then nothing happens. It's worse than when he first went in. At least then I knew it was going to be a long time.

The Problem

The parole process is hard to understand. Often the rules are unclear and at the end of the prison term it seems like everything is up in the air. It's possible you won't know anything until he is actually out. Prison officials don't seem to consider families when they make decisions about release.

It's like you're on a seesaw. You take turns, first hoping and then giving up hope until you just feel drained. Some women simply refuse to get their hopes up because they're afraid they'll only be disappointed again. But at the same time it's important to prepare for his homecoming and you can't do that if you refuse to think about it or plan for it.

During this time it's hard to know what to tell the kids. They've had their father taken away once without any warning. You hate to see them get their hopes up now until you're sure about the release. You don't want to see them hurt any more.

Ideas and Suggestions

If your guy has served a short term with no write-ups, it's almost certain that he'll get parole and he doesn't need a lawyer.

41

Usually he will meet with the parole board several months before he is actually paroled. In some states he may be given a brief furlough for job-hunting and a visit home before he finally is allowed to come home for good.

If he's served a long term, had write-ups, tried to escape, or is having a clemency hearing, things will be more complicated and it's a good idea to have a lawyer. If you can't afford to pay one, check with the Public Defender's office or Legal Aid. If they can't help you themselves, they can usually refer you to someone who can.

Sometimes nonprofit agencies that work with prisoners will offer help in getting ready for parole hearings. They may also know good lawyers willing to work for free or for "$10 a week forever." They're good people to talk to. Since parole board hearings are open to the public in most states, you may want to sit through a couple of hearings beforehand, just so you'll know what they're like.

In most states it's a good idea to attend your husband's parole hearing yourself, along with your starched and shiny kids. It's good for the board to see that the prisoner has a supportive family to return to. If for some reason you cannot be there, write a letter to the parole board explaining why you aren't there and how much you would *like* to be there. Explain in your own words why you think your husband should be released now and how much you're looking forward to having him back home. You might enclose a snapshot of the family, again to show that a supportive family is waiting.

It's also usually helpful for relatives and neighbors who would be good character references to attend the hearing. If there's a former employer willing to hire your husband back, do your best to get that employer to the hearing. If he can't come, take a letter from him, even if you have to write it yourself and have the employer sign it. Your minister would also be a good witness. In some states prison employees, including chaplins and counselors, may also be allowed to speak on behalf of a prisoner.

CAUTION: Be careful about a lawyer who is eager to represent you before a parole board for a big fee, especially if he or she wants to be paid in advance. An eager beaver who's into paroles for profit may not be a good lawyer. You may also run into a person, usually *not* a lawyer, who claims to be able to influence the parole board or the governor to let your partner out if you're willing to pay a fee. This is one of the oldest rackets around prisons and should be reported to the authorities. Try to remember that lawyers who *really* understand how parole works are not usually in it for the money.

While you can help and encourage him from the outside, your partner has the main responsibility in getting ready for parole. If he doesn't make it the first time, remember that he'll get another chance, maybe in six months. If it seems pretty chancy the first time round, why not look on it as a rehearsal and tell your kids that. Then, if he does get out, it's a fantastic surprise for all of you. It's a lot easier to handle that way than getting a "no" when you expect a "yes!"

Some Questions

•How can I find out what's going on about his parole and release?

•What should I say to my children about when he will get out?

•Is there anything I can do to make the parole board or the courts grant his release?

•What can I do about my own up and down seesaw feelings?

Half Way Home

We'd both been so sure Jack would make parole. I even decided not to take time off to go to his hearing. With the kids starting back to school in a couple of weeks, we were going to need every cent of that paycheck! But now I'm scared. I've never seen Jack looking so glum at visiting hours!

"Yeah, I made it—in a manner of speaking," he said. "I can leave here in September, but I can't come home. They've got me down for some halfway house—alcohol and drug stuff. That'll probably be worse than prison!"

43

The Problem

You and the kids have been looking forward to having Jack home and, to be honest, you've also been looking forward to another paycheck. Before he went in he lost a couple of jobs drinking, but he was a good enough welder to get another job fast and he brought home good money.

You also remember the times when he roughed you up and was pretty hard on the kids. But that was three years ago. You've been hoping things would be different now and maybe with the halfway house they will be. In the past you learned to grab the good stuff quick, before someone took it away. That's how you've waited for Jack, expecting that sooner or later things will fall apart again. Only maybe this time things *will* be different.

Ideas and Suggestions:

It's hard not to worry about Jack. He's given you *reason!* But all of us find it easier to act like grown-ups when we're treated like grown-ups. It's time for you to become a team again. Maybe you need to assume that Jack is an adult member of the family team and ask his advice about things.

When drugs and alcohol have been a problem, it will be easier for Jack if both of you can stay away from drinking and drugs. When he finally does get home, don't keep beer in the refrigerator. Try to find fun-time activities that don't make you think of drinking. Keep some hot chocolate mix on hand for bedtime snacks. Plan a candle-light dinner for two with mineral water and a slice of lemon. (Easy on the budget, too.)

But what if Jack does goof? Will it be the end of the world or will he be able to put things back together? He's been abusing substances for a long, long time and he could slip up. If he does, it's his problem to handle. Your job is to reassure him by expressing lots of confidence in him, not to be his mama who will solve all his problems.

On the other hand, Jack probably can't handle superhuman things like working an eighty-hour week. If he tries to make his body do more than a human body can do, it's only natural that he will start thinking about speed or meth. If he feels like he owes his family a whole lot, and he *does*, it's easy for him to expect himself to do the impossible. Maybe some gentle kidding from you can help. "Hey, it's you I love, not Superman!"

Some Questions

•Will the drug and alcohol treatment really help?
•Can I count on him not to abuse us after he gets home?
•Should I have a backup plan in case things fall apart again?

Life Goes On

The sun makes shadow patterns on the path as Jennifer and I walk through the zoo. Her face is glowing as she watches the bear cubs play. Our weekends together have been really special lately. Full of curiosity and enthusiasm, she asks question after question, just like when she used to come here with her father.

That stops me short. Should we be having this much fun? Am I filling in for dad too well? I know that Daniel would like to be here with us. He is missing so much. Sometimes it seems we should try to make time stand still until he gets home.

Maybe I should remind Jennifer that we're not really a family now. But that doesn't seem fair, either. It would put a real damper on our day, and this day is too precious for painful reminders.

The Problem

Your life goes on. You learn to enjoy being a family even though one very important member is missing. You *know* that he will come back and that some things will have to change when he comes. But you can't stop living in the meantime. There's no telling *when* he'll be back.

There are times when you stop suddenly and realize you are managing just fine without him. That's scary because it makes you wonder how you will make a place for him when he comes back into your life. You may even feel guilty that you don't miss him all the time. The good part of this is that it also lets you forget some of the pain for a while. You don't want to keep feeling the pain just so you can feel it stop hurting when he finally comes home again.

Ideas and Suggestions

Kids really do grow up only once. Time won't stand still, no matter how much we would like it to sometimes. Your partner isn't just missing a lot of *fun,* he's also not home to share the *responsibility.* When things go wrong, you have to take care of it.

These years need to hold as much happiness and growth as possible for all of you—your kids, your partner, and yourself. Being locked up surely isn't fun, but there are probably some chances for education or vocational training in prison.

Your partner has buddies, and maybe the chance of an occasional softball game on a sunny day. You probably don't get much free time, what with holding down a job and raising a family single-handedly. How about *you* having a little fun or getting a chance to learn something new?

While you and your family are growing on the outside, how can you share enough of your life with your partner so that he will continue to feel like a close member of the family? Do you have an inexpensive camera? Send him some snapshots! Could Jennifer send him some of her school papers, and make him cards for all the holidays? It may be the only Columbus Day card he'll get in his life!

Some Questions

- Should we change the way we are living so that we keep a place for him?
- How far ahead should we plan for his return?
- What should I tell the children about when daddy will come home?
- If we begin to really enjoy life without him, will the children resent him when he comes in and makes everything change?

Chapter 4

Homecoming

Late at night it's the hardest. You are used to snuggling and you got nobody to snuggle to. And pillows just don't get it. They don't keep you as warm—they don't generate heat.

Finally, he's home! Only things are different than they have ever been before and you have to learn to be a family all over again.

You need to learn to be together again as lovers. You need to learn new ways of being parents and children together. You need to be together as two strong and responsible adults who are committed to making your family work.

Things will never be the way they once were, but maybe they can be better.

Being Lovers Again

It's strange to feel someone in bed with me again. I know Rob is awake. I feel his body stiff beside me.

"Rob, please don't be mad at me. I don't want you to be cross."

"All I wanted was a little loving, that's all! I've been gone for years, and now that I'm home I just get the cold shoulder!"

"Just give me time. I need some time. You're so demanding! Sometimes in the last week I've felt like I was living with an animal. Is sex all you think about?"

The Problem

You've been apart for a long time. He has thought about you and you about him. You have both imagined what it would be like to be together again. Only, it doesn't go as smoothly as you imagined. Maybe you haven't both imagined it the same way. In some ways you're like strangers again and it takes time to get to know each other.

Neither of you wants to wait. You want to make love again, like you used to. But you're used to sleeping alone. You've had privacy and your own schedule. Now he's there with you. He has thought about having sex with you for a long time and he is in your bed, demanding your body. It's hard to get used to and nothing seems to go the way you thought it would.

Ideas and Suggestions

Sexual adjustments are never easy. First you and your partner are torn apart and now he's back in your bed. It is important to talk about sex when you are not involved in the passion of the act itself.

He will love to hear that you missed his body and thought of your lovemaking while he was gone. Tell him during the day and talk about how you feel and what you want.

It is always better to have sex when you are relaxed—not when you have just had a fight about the kids or money. It may be a good idea for you both to agree to that in your daytime discussions so that sex does not become a way for you to avoid problems or to gloss over conflict. To "kiss and make up" when you haven't faced the real problem can create a lot of bad feelings later on.

One important thing about sex is that it should be fun. It should be a time when you can let go of adult responsibilities and become like two playful children again. Sex is an inexpensive way to enjoy time together!

Finally, there must be give and take. Remember he has been longing for you as much as you have for him. Be willing to give a little even when you are not fully in the mood so that the next time you need some good loving you can feel free to ask for it.

Some Questions

- Do I have to have sex whenever he wants me to?
- How can I understand his sexual needs?
- How can I tell him what I want and how I feel?
- Is it asking too much to want him to wait until I get used to having him around again?
- Why can't he think about anything besides sex?

Who Pays the Bills?

"I'll see you tonight, Sam. I'm leaving now. There's some money in my top dresser drawer. Help yourself if you need any."

"Sure, help myself to *your* money. Who do you think you are, the Queen of Sheba? I'd rather go broke than live on handouts from you!"

Suddenly I feel just like I do with the kids when they are being selfish and demanding. The weariness of the last years and months washes over me again. I don't know what to do. I just know I have to leave because I have to get to work.

I'm the one who makes the money now. He's looking for a job but it's not easy for an ex-con to get work. Maybe I should just quit my job. Lord knows I'm tired of getting up and going to work every day. Then *he* would have to take care of us. Maybe he'd like that better!

The Problem

Life has gone on while your partner was in prison. You did what was necessary to keep the family going. You made it on your own.

But now he's back and he doesn't know how he fits in. Maybe he feels useless, especially if he doesn't have a job so he can provide for the family. He's not used to staying home while *you* go out to work, and he may resent it if he hasn't thought about it carefully ahead of time. Maybe he feels weak and unimportant because he's not taking care of his family.

These feelings can create real problems between you. He may think you're being so independent that you don't really need him. Maybe he will accuse you of trying to run the show. He may just get depressed and angry at you.

Sometimes your partner may wish that things could be just the way they used to be in the "old days." He sees how everything has changed and he may even tell you that he liked you better the way you used to be, before all this happened.

There are times when that even sounds good to you. You're so tired that part of you would almost like somebody else to take over. But another part of you doesn't want to go back because it feels good to be able to take care of things.

In fact, it seems kind of *unfair* that he hasn't said anything about how well you've kept things together while he was gone. It'd be nice if he could show a little appreciation. Only, maybe he can't because then he'd be admitting that you can get along without him.

Ideas and Suggestions

He created a great big problem for the family and you had to take care of it. It would take an unusually grown-up guy to admit that, even to himself, let alone to tell you "Thanks."

He's also not going to thank you for coming up with long lists of places for him to apply for a job. If there's an agency in your city that helps people find jobs when they leave prison, you could mention it. Or maybe one or two practically surefire bets for a job, if you've heard of any. But keep it low key. "I ran into Chuck and he asked me to tell you," or something like that. Tell him and then shut up, even if he doesn't rush right down to apply. Nagging will only hurt the situation.

You don't want your partner unhappy because you're trying to run his show. It would be even worse if he should learn to like it. What you don't need is another child, six foot tall, around the house!

When it comes to money, keep things matter-of-fact. If you've always considered money "family money," remind him of that. "Sometimes *you* earn it, sometimes *I* earn it and sometimes we *both* earn it. We use it together, carefully right now, because it has to stretch a long way!"

And what do you get out of it? The two of you, with the kids, are building good lives together in the community. Having fun. Being a family. It's what you've been dreaming of, the dream you hoped would come true. There ought to be some reward for keeping a family going and coping while someone's in prison. Maybe *part* of that reward is feeling how strong you've become.

Some Questions

- How can I stay strong, the way I am now, and still let him know that I care about him?
- Should I stand up for myself when he gets angry at me or just let it be?
- Should we think about arranging for some professional counseling?

Being Parents Again, Together

"Danny, I told you not to stay over at the neighbors so long. What you need is a good thrashing! I'll bet you haven't been spanked since I went away!"

"Stop it, Stan! Danny's a good kid. He's had to learn a lot of responsibility while you were gone. He knows when he needs to be in. We have an understanding."

"An *understanding!* I see! And I'm not part of that understanding, huh? I guess I might just as well keep my mouth shut! I don't have anything to say about what my kids do!"

The Problem

Children depend on routines. Their lives need to have a pattern that they can count on. They need to learn to know their limits and to understand what is expected of them. They need to be guided in this by their parents. When one parent is gone for a long time it is only natural that they will take their cues from the parent who is home with them.

This can lead to some serious confusion when the missing parent returns. The parents may give mixed signals while they learn to parent as a team, again.

One of the things that parents in prison miss most of all is watching their children develop. When they come home they often find that their children have grown up and are almost strangers to them. Seeing this reminds them again of what they have missed. It may make them angry. Maybe they'll want to make up for lost time. They may try to take over instead of taking the time to learn to know their kids again.

Ideas and Suggestions

If you live close enough to the prison to visit your partner often, you can probably also take the kids, at least *some* of the time. If he sees them often, he will have a much better idea of what is going on in their lives when he is released. Even so, visiting is a lot different than being back home with them. There's nobody small to bathe or tuck in at night in the visiting gallery!

Some decisions can be made together even when your partner is still *in* prison. You can ask him what he thinks about Danny's hearing. Does he agree that it may be a good idea to have it checked? Michelle's been asked for a date. Can she possibly be old enough? Because he isn't with them all the time, he may notice changes and problems that you have missed.

Sometimes a father wasn't so good with the kids even before he went to prison. If he didn't have much love himself while he was growing up, he may find it tough to be a parent. But parenting is a skill that can usually be learned, and some prisons even sponsor parenting classes for men in prison. That's worth looking into.

One thing is for sure. Kids don't stop growing while their father is locked up. It's important for him to be aware of *how* they are growing so that when he comes home he is prepared for their more grown-up privileges.

Some Questions

- How can we divide the responsibility for the kids so we're not always tangling over it?
- How can we explain to the children what's happening?
- Should I just go away and leave him alone with them for a while?
- Can I trust him to take care of them?
- When is the best time to talk about the kids?
- Is there anything I can do to help him get to know the kids again?

Going Straight

"Where are you going, Ken? You were gone pretty late last night. I hope you won't stay out so late tonight."

"What are you, my *keeper?* When I got out of jail I got away

54

from guards. Don't you start in on me! Maybe you think I'm just a kid!"

"Ken, I'm worried about you. I just don't want it to happen all over again. Please, let me know everything is all right. I just don't want anything to happen to you."

The Problem

It's never easy to forget the past, especially the painful past. So the hurt of having had your partner in prison hangs around for a long time.

When he does come home it's only natural for you to be scared that the whole thing will happen again. You worry about him hanging around with his old friends and you're scared that he may drink too much again. Then you start to feel like it's up to you to keep it from happening. You'd like to be able to trust him, but your worrying gets in the way. Sometimes you *do* feel more like a mother than a partner.

A person who's been under lock and key for a couple of years may not be able to handle that kind of worrying. It's possible that he really can't understand your concern. Maybe it's even hard for you to sit and talk about it without seeming suspicious of him.

Ideas and Suggestions

This is *tough*. Usually, people who are trusted try to deserve that trust. But if a man feels like his partner is a policewoman, he may try to see how much he can get away with.

On the other hand, you do need to know what goes on. It could take your partner less than twenty minutes to get himself back in trouble. If he starts drinking or hanging around with an old friend you know is bad news, or if he seems depressed, you need to *do* something.

For many couples the answer could be a nice evening together at home, or somewhere else where you can talk. You don't need to have all the answers, just be ready to listen and encourage.

You might also make a point of just spending more time with him, if he'd like that. Even when you don't think you can afford a baby-sitter so you can go along bowling, it may be a good investment.

In the end, though, you have to let go. It's up to your partner to decide to stay out of trouble and to choose the kind of life he wants. It's something *he* has to want and do for himself. You can help by being good company and providing lots of love and encouragement. Beyond that you can only pray that he will make the choices that will make it possible for you to build a better life together.

Some Questions

•How can I tell him what I feel without making him angry?
•How can we learn to trust each other again?
•How much should I know about what he does when he is not with me?
•Would it help us to talk with someone else about this problem?

Conclusions

I'll show people pictures and some have said to me, "Gosh, he looks like a real person." That's terrible.

Conclusions

Families of prisoners are doing time just like those actually in prison. They have to live with the pain of separation, usually without the support of the church or community. Although they face years of grief and heartache, they go almost completely unnoticed by the society around them.

In this booklet we have traced the experience of families of prisoners through the first days, into the first year, over the long haul, and finally right up to the homecoming. The stories are the stories of unique individuals. They are all different. Yet they are the same in that they all share in the pain of being connected to a man in prison.

Women faced with the loss of a partner are forced to cope with the changes and difficulties that always follow such loss. These difficulties can be as small as comforting a child who misses daddy or as huge as choosing a new career. Whatever the problem, the family will have to find new resources to stay alive.

This booklet is offered as one resource for families who face this situation. We hope that it will help them to know that they are not alone, that there are other people who have lived through the pain. We also hope that this booklet will encourage people who live with and around families of prisoners to understand their special needs and to offer a helping hand.

We believe that communities cannot be whole and healthy places as long as there are people in them who are ignored or misunderstood. This booklet is an attempt to share the stories of some of the people in our communities who have been overlooked so that healing can begin.

Some Resources

I love him. It's as simple as that. I'm waiting for him to come home.

Some Resources

Services for Families of Offenders: An Overview (book)
Excellent overview of the issues facing families of prisoners. Includes addresses of a number of established programs; also a review of the literature and a bibliography. By Susan Hoffman Fishman and Candace Cassin, 1981. Stock number 024-000-01126-8 available for $3.25 from the Superintendent of Documents, US Government Printing Office, Washington, DC 20402

Directory of Programs Serving Families of Adult Offenders (booklet)
Lists programs and their services in 22 states and some Canadian provinces. By Jim Mustin, June 1985. Available at no charge from National Institute of Corrections Information Center, 1790 30th Street, Suite 130, Boulder, CO 80301; (303-444-1101).

Family and Corrections Network Working Papers (newsletter)
Publishes quarterly selected reprints of articles about programs serving families involved in the criminal justice system. For subscription information contact James W. Mustin, Editor, *FCN Working Papers,* P.O. Box 2103, Waynesboro, VA 22980.

"I know how you feel, because it happened to me" (book)
A Handbook for Kids with a Parent in Prison
Useful for children as well as for adults working with children whose parents are in prison. A project of Prison Match in 1984, the book is available for $3.50 from Prison Match, 1515 Webster St. #403, Oakland, CA 94612; (415-763-0518).

Prison Match: Programs for Children and Inmate Parents (program)
A nonprofit agency operating a multi-service children's center inside the Federal Correctional Institution in Pleasanton, California. Prison Match has developed resources for both parents and children and can provide technical assistance to others interested in building programs for children with parents in prison. For information contact Prison Match, 1515 Webster St. #403, Oakland, CA 94612; (415-763-0518).

Friends Outside (program)
Services to families of prisoners include outreach to families, hospitality centers offering overnight lodging and child care, transportation,

counseling, holiday activities, women's support groups, and children's activities. Most chapters are in California, a few also in Nevada and Idaho. Check your phone book for a chapter in your community or contact Friends Outside National Office, 404 Lincoln Ave., Salinas CA 93901; (408-758-2733).

Prison Families Anonymous (program)

A self-help organization that offers information and emotional support in court and jail lobbies, weekly support groups to enable families to cope with day-to-day survival, and groups to help children deal with their feelings about themselves and their incarcerated parent. For information contact Prison Families Anonymous, 91 N. Franklin St., Room 304, Hempstead, NY 11550; (516-538-6065).

Waiting on the Outside (play)

A play based on the experiences of women whose partners are in prison. May be booked as a live performance or on videotape which is available to rent or purchase. Contact Bridgework Theater, 113½ East Lincoln, Goshen, IN 46526; (219-534-1085).

Waiting on the Outside (photo exhibit)

A traveling exhibit of black-and-white portraits and quotations from women whose partners are prisoners or ex-prisoners. Also includes a reading that was written for use in a worship setting. Available on loan for $5.00 from Mennonite Central Committee Office of Criminal Justice, 220 West High, Elkhart, IN 46516; (219-293-3090).